This Land is My Land

# Table of Contents

Map: 1920—Original territory assigned to the Jewish National Home ................ 1
Map: 1922—Final territory assigned to the Jewish National Home ..................... 1
"In Palestine as of right and not on sufferance" ......................................................... 2
Introduction ................................................................................................................... 4
The legal aspects of Jewish rights to a National Home in Palestine ....................... 5
The two most significant events in modern history leading to the creation
of the Jewish National Home ...................................................................................... 5
The founding of modern Zionism ................................................................................ 5
The Balfour Declaration ................................................................................................ 5
The origin and nature of the "Mandate for Palestine" .............................................. 6
Recognition of historical connection to Palestine ..................................................... 7
Map: Jewish Palestine ................................................................................................... 8
Palestine is a geographical area, not a nationality ..................................................... 9
There has never been a sovereign Arab state in Palestine ...................................... 11
The "Mandate" defined where Jews are and are not permitted to settle ............. 12
Political rights in Palestine were granted to Jews only .......................................... 13
Jewish Peoplehood in Palestine ................................................................................. 14
Jerusalem in "Mandate" time .................................................................................... 14
Jewish rights to Palestine were internationally guaranteed .................................. 15
United States Government and the "Mandate" policy .......................................... 16
The "Mandate for Palestine" is valid to this day ..................................................... 17
Futile efforts to challenge the "Mandate for Palestine" ......................................... 19
Myth: The "Mandate for Palestine" is a Class "A" Mandate ................................. 19
Myth: The "Mandate" violates Article 22 of the Covenant of the League ........... 20
Myth: Palestine was promised to the Arabs by Sir Henry McMahon ................. 22
Myth: The 1949 "Green Line" is Israel's internationally recognized border ....... 23
Myth: Palestinian Arabs seek peace with Israel ...................................................... 24
Appendix A - The "Mandate for Palestine" ............................................................. 25
Appendix B - Article 25 of the "Palestine Mandate" was realized ....................... 33
Appendix C - Article 22 of the Covenant of the League of Nations ..................... 35
Appendix D - UN Resolution 181 – Recommendation to partition ..................... 37
Map: The Recommendation to Partition Palestine ................................................. 38
Appendix E - Israel's Declaration of Independence ............................................... 44
"Redemption of Palestine" ......................................................................................... 46
Appendix F - Israel's Government position ............................................................ 47
Notes ............................................................................................................................. 48

# Introduction

Ever ask yourself why during the 30 year period—between 1917 and 1947— thousands of Jews throughout the world woke up one morning and decided to leave their homes and go to Palestine? The majority did this because they heard that a future National Home for the Jewish people was being established in Palestine, on the basis of the League of Nations obligation under the "Mandate for Palestine" document.

The "Mandate for Palestine," an historical League of Nations document, laid down the Jewish legal right to settle anywhere in western Palestine, between the Jordan River and the Mediterranean Sea, an entitlement unaltered in international law.

The "Mandate for Palestine" was not a naive vision briefly embraced by the international community. Fifty-one member countries—the entire League of Nations—unanimously declared on July 24, 1922:

> "Whereas recognition has been given to the historical connection of the Jewish people with Palestine and to the grounds for reconstituting their national home in that country."

It is important to point out that political rights to self-determination as a polity for Arabs were guaranteed by the same League of Nations in four other mandates—in Lebanon and Syria (The French Mandate), Iraq, and later Trans-Jordan [The British Mandate].

Any attempt to negate the Jewish people's right to Palestine—*Eretz-Israel*, and to deny them access and control in the area designated for the Jewish people by the League of Nations is a serious infringement of international law.

> The "Road Map" vision, as well as continuous pressure from the "Quartet" (U.S., the European Union, the UN and Russia) to surrender parts of *Eretz-Israel* are contrary to international law that firmly call to "encourage ... close settlement by Jews on the land, including State lands and waste lands not required for public purposes." It also requires the Mandatory for "seeing that no Palestine territory shall be ceded or leased to, or in any way placed under the control of the government of any foreign power."

In their attempt to establish peace between the Jewish state and its Arab neighbors, the nations of the world should remember who the lawful sovereign is with its rights anchored in international law, valid to this day: The Jewish Nation.

And in support of the Jewish people, I sat down and wrote this pamphlet.

Eli E. Hertz

# The Legal Aspects of Jewish Rights to a National Home in Palestine

## The Two Most Significant Events in Modern History Leading to the Creation of the Jewish National Home:

### I. The Founding of Modern Zionism
Benjamin Ze'ev (Theodor) Herzl (May 2, 1860 – July 3, 1904)

After witnessing the spread of antisemitism around the world, Herzl felt compelled to create a political movement with the goal of establishing a Jewish National Home in Palestine. To this end, he assembled the first Zionist Congress in Basel, Switzerland, in 1897. Herzl's insights and vision can be learned from his writings:

> "Oppression and persecution cannot exterminate us. No nation on earth has survived such struggles and sufferings as we have gone through.

> "Palestine is our ever-memorable historic home. The very name of Palestine would attract our people with a force of marvelous potency.

> "The idea which I have developed in this pamphlet is a very old one: it is the restoration of the Jewish State.

> "The world resounds with outcries against the Jews, and these outcries have awakened the slumbering idea. ... We are a people—one people."[1]

### II. The Balfour Declaration
The British Foreign Office, November 2, 1917

Dear Lord Rothschild,

I have much pleasure in conveying to you, on behalf of His Majesty's Government, the following declaration of sympathy with Jewish Zionist aspirations which has been submitted to, and approved by, the Cabinet.

> "His Majesty's Government view with favour the establishment in Palestine of a national home for the Jewish people, and will use their best endeavours to facilitate the achievement of this object, it being clearly understood that nothing shall be done which may prejudice the civil and religious rights of existing non-Jewish communities in Palestine, or the rights and political status enjoyed by Jews in any other country."

I should be grateful if you would bring this declaration to the knowledge of the Zionist Federation.[2]

Signed,
Arthur James Balfour
[Secretary of State for Foreign Affairs]

## The Origin and Nature of the "Mandate for Palestine"

The "Mandate for Palestine," an historical League of Nations document, laid down the Jewish legal right to settle anywhere in western Palestine, a 10,000-square-miles[3] area between the Jordan River and the Mediterranean Sea.

The legally binding document was conferred on April 24, 1920 at the San Remo Conference, and its terms outlined in the Treaty of Sèvres on August 10, 1920. The Mandate's terms were finalized and unanimously approved on July 24, 1922, by the Council of the League of Nations, which was comprised at that time of 51 countries[4], and became operational on September 29, 1923.[5]

The "Mandate for Palestine" was not a naive vision briefly embraced by the international community in blissful unawareness of Arab opposition to the very notion of Jewish historical rights in Palestine. The Mandate weathered the test of time: On April 18, 1946, when the League of Nations was dissolved and its assets and duties transferred to the United Nations, the international community, in essence, reaffirmed the validity of this international accord and reconfirmed that the terms for a Jewish National Home were the will of the international community, a "sacred trust" – despite the fact that by then it was patently clear that the Arabs opposed a Jewish National Home, no matter what the form.

> Many seem to confuse the "Mandate for Palestine" [The Trust], with the British Mandate [The Trustee]. The "Mandate for Palestine" is a League of Nations document that laid down the Jewish legal rights in Palestine. The British Mandate, on the other hand, was entrusted by the League of Nations with the responsibility to administrate the area delineated by the "Mandate for Palestine."

Great Britain [i.e., the Mandatory or Trustee] did turn over its responsibility to the United Nations as of May 14, 1948. However, the legal force of the League of Nations' "Mandate for Palestine" [i.e., The Trust] was not terminated with the end of the British Mandate. Rather, the Trust was transferred over to the United Nations.

## Recognition of the Historical Connection to Palestine

Fifty-one member countries – the entire League of Nations – unanimously declared on July 24, 1922:

> "Whereas recognition has been given to the historical connection of the Jewish people with Palestine and to the grounds for reconstituting their national home in that country."[6]

Unlike nation-states in Europe, modern Lebanese, Jordanian, Syrian, and Iraqi nationalities did not evolve. They were arbitrarily created by colonial powers.

In 1919, in the wake of World War I, England and France as Mandatory (e.g., official administrators and mentors) carved up the former Ottoman Empire, which had collapsed a year earlier, into geographic spheres of influence. This divided the Mideast into new political entities with new names and frontiers.[7]

Territory was divided along map meridians without regard for traditional frontiers (i.e., geographic logic and sustainability) or the ethnic composition of indigenous populations.[8]

The prevailing rationale behind these artificially created states was how they served the imperial and commercial needs of their colonial masters. Iraq and Jordan, for instance, were created as emirates to reward the noble Hashemite family from Saudi Arabia for its loyalty to the British against the Ottoman Turks during World War I, under the leadership of Lawrence of Arabia. Iraq was given to Faisal bin Hussein, son of the sheriff of Mecca, in 1918. To reward his younger brother Abdullah with an emirate, Britain cut away 77 percent of its mandate over Palestine earmarked for the Jews and gave it to Abdullah in 1922, creating the new country of Trans-Jordan or Jordan, as it was later named.

The Arabs' hatred of the Jewish State has never been strong enough to prevent the bloody rivalries that repeatedly rock the Middle East. These conflicts were evident in the civil wars in Yemen and Lebanon, as well as in the war between Iraq and Iran, in the gassing of countless Kurds in Iraq, and in the killing of Iraqis by Iraqis.

The manner in which European colonial powers carved out political entities with little regard to their ethnic composition not only led to this inter-ethnic violence, but it also encouraged dictatorial rule as the only force capable of holding such entities together.[9]

The exception was Palestine, or Eretz-Israel – the territory between the Jordan River and the Mediterranean Sea, where:

> "The Mandatory shall be responsible for placing the country [Palestine] under such political, administrative and economic conditions as will secure the establishment of the Jewish National Home, as laid down in the preamble, and the development of self-governing institutions, and also for safeguarding the civil and religious rights of all the inhabitants of Palestine, irrespective of race and religion."[10]

## Jewish Palestine

## Palestine is a Geographical Area, Not a Nationality

Delineating the final geographical area of Palestine designated for the Jewish National Home on September 16, 1922, as described by the Mandatory:[11]

> PALESTINE
> INTRODUCTORY.
> POSITION, ETC.
>
> Palestine lies on the western edge of the continent of Asia between Latitude 30º N. and 33º N., Longitude 34º 30' E. and 35º 30' E.
>
> On the North it is bounded by the French Mandated Territories of Syria and Lebanon, on the East by Syria and Trans-Jordan, on the South-west by the Egyptian province of Sinai, on the South-east by the Gulf of Aqaba and on the West by the Mediterranean. The frontier with Syria was laid down by the Anglo-French Convention of the 23rd December, 1920, and its delimitation was ratified in 1923. Briefly stated, the boundaries are as follows:
>
> *North.*—From Ras en Naqura on the Mediterranean eastwards to a point west of Qadas, thence in a northerly direction to Metulla, thence east to a point west of Banias.
>
> *East.*—From Banias in a southerly direction east of Lake Hula to Jisr Banat Ya'pub, thence along a line east of the Jordan and the Lake of Tiberias and on to El Hamme station on the Samakh-Deraa railway line, thence along the centre of the river Yarmuq to its confluence with the Jordan, thence along the centres of the Jordan, the Dead Sea and the Wadi Araba to a point on the Gulf of Aqaba two miles west of the town of Aqaba, thence along the shore of the Gulf of Aqaba to Ras Jaba.
>
> *South.*—From Ras Jaba in a generally north-westerly direction to the junction of the Neki-Aqaba and Gaza-Aqaba Roads, thence to a point west-north-west of Ain Maghara and thence to a point on the Mediterranean coast north-west of Rafa.
>
> *West.*—The Mediterranean Sea.

Arabs, the UN and its organs, and lately the International Court of Justice (ICJ) as well, have repeatedly claimed that the Palestinians are a native people—so much so that almost everyone takes it for granted. The problem is that a stateless Palestinian people is a fabrication. The word Palestine is not even Arabic.[12]

In a report by His Majesty's Government in the United Kingdom of Great Britain and Northern Ireland to the Council of the League of Nations on the administration of Palestine and Trans-Jordan for the year 1938, the British made it clear: Palestine is not a state, it is the name of a geographical area.[13]

Palestine is a name coined by the Romans around 135 CE from the name of a seagoing Aegean people who settled on the coast of Canaan in antiquity—the *Philistines*. The name was chosen to replace Judea, as a sign that Jewish sovereignty had been eradicated following the Jewish Revolts against Rome.

In the course of time, the Latin name *Philistia* was further bastardized into *Palistina* or *Palestine*.[14] During the next 2,000 years Palestine was never an independent state belonging to any people, nor did a Palestinian people distinct from other Arabs appear during 1,300 years of Muslim hegemony in Palestine under Arab and Ottoman rule. During that rule, local Arabs were actually considered part of, and subject to, the authority of Greater Syria (*Suriyya al-Kubra*).[15]

Historically, before the Arabs fabricated the concept of Palestinian peoplehood as an exclusively Arab phenomenon, no such group existed. This is substantiated in countless official British Mandate-vintage documents that speak of the *Jews and the Arabs of Palestine*—not Jews and Palestinians.[16]

In fact, before local Jews began calling themselves Israelis in 1948 (when the name "Israel" was chosen for the newly-established Jewish State), the term "Palestine" applied almost exclusively to Jews and the institutions founded by new Jewish immigrants in the first half of the 20th century, before the state's independence.

Some examples include:

- The Jerusalem Post, founded in 1932, was called The Palestine Post until 1948.
- Bank Leumi L'Israel, incorporated in 1902, was called the Anglo-Palestine Company until 1948.
- The Jewish Agency, an arm of the Zionist movement engaged in Jewish settlement since 1929, was initially called the Jewish Agency for Palestine.
- Today's Israel Philharmonic Orchestra, founded in 1936 by German Jewish refugees who fled Nazi Germany, was originally called the Palestine Symphony Orchestra, composed of some 70 Palestinian Jews.[17]
- The United Jewish Appeal (UJA) was established in 1939 as a merger of the United Palestine Appeal and the fund-raising arm of the Joint Distribution Committee.

Encouraged by their success at historical revisionism and brainwashing the world with the "Big Lie" of a Palestinian people, Palestinian Arabs have more recently begun to claim they are the descendants of the Philistines and even the Stone Age Canaanites.[18] Based on that myth, they can claim to have been "victimized" twice by the Jews: in the conquest of Canaan by the Israelites and again by the Israelis in modern times - a total fabrication.[19] Archeologists explain that the Philistines were a Mediterranean people who settled along the coast of Canaan in 1100 BCE. They have no connection to the Arab nation, a desert people who emerged from the Arabian Peninsula.

As if that myth were not enough, former PLO Chairman Yasir Arafat also claimed, "Palestinian Arabs are descendants of the Jebusites," who were displaced when King David conquered Jerusalem.

Arafat also argued that "Abraham was an Iraqi." One Christmas Eve, Arafat declared that "Jesus was a Palestinian," a preposterous claim that echoes the words of Hanan Ashrawi, a Christian Arab who, in an interview during the 1991 Madrid Conference, said: "Jesus Christ was born in my country, in my land," and claimed that she was "the descendant of the first Christians," disciples who spread the gospel around Bethlehem some 600 years before the Arab conquest. If her claims were true, it would be tantamount to confessing that she is a Jew!

Contradictions abound; Palestinian leaders claim to be descended from the Canaanites, the Philistines, the Jebusites and the first Christians. They also "hijacked" Jesus and ignored his Jewishness, at the same time claiming the Jews never were a people and never built the Holy Temples in Jerusalem.

## There Has Never Been a Sovereign Arab State in Palestine

The artificiality of a Palestinian identity is reflected in the attitudes and actions of neighboring Arab nations who never established a Palestinian state themselves.

The rhetoric by Arab leaders on behalf of the Palestinians rings hollow. Arabs in neighboring states, who control 99.9 percent of the Middle East land, have never recognized a Palestinian entity. They have always considered Palestine and its inhabitants part of the great "Arab nation," historically and politically as an integral part of Greater Syria – *Suriyya al-Kubra* – a designation that extended to both sides of the Jordan River.[20] In the 1950s, Jordan simply annexed the West Bank since the population there was viewed as the brethren of the Jordanians. Jordan's official narrative of "Jordanian state-building" attests to this fact:

> "Jordanian identity underlies the significant and fundamental common denominator that makes it inclusive of Palestinian identity, particularly in view of the shared historic social and political development of the people on both sides of the Jordan. ... The Jordan government, in view of the historical and political relationship with the West Bank ... granted all Palestinian refugees on its territory full citizenship rights while protecting and upholding their political rights as Palestinians (Right of Return or compensation)."[21]

The Arabs never established a Palestinian state when the UN in 1947 recommended to partition Palestine, and to establish "an Arab and a Jewish state" (not a Palestinian state, it should be noted). Nor did the Arabs recognize or establish a Palestinian state *during the two decades prior to the Six-Day War* when the West Bank was under Jordanian control and the Gaza Strip was under Egyptian control; nor did the Palestinian Arabs clamor for autonomy or independence during those years under Jordanian and Egyptian rule.

And as for Jerusalem: Only twice in the city's history has it served as a national capital. First as the capital of the two Jewish Commonwealths during the First and Second Temple periods, as described in the Bible, reinforced by archaeological evidence and numerous ancient documents. And again in modern times as the capital of the State of Israel. It has never served as an Arab capital for the simple reason that there has never been a Palestinian Arab state.

Well before the 1967 decision to create a new Arab people called "Palestinians," when the word "Palestinian" was associated with Jewish endeavors, Auni Bey Abdul-Hadi, a local Arab leader, testified in 1937 before the Peel Commission, a British investigative body:

> "There is no such country [as Palestine]! Palestine is a term the Zionists invented! There is no Palestine in the Bible. Our country was for centuries, part of Syria."[22]

In a 1946 appearance before the Anglo-American Committee of Inquiry, also acting as an investigative body, the Arab-American historian Philip Hitti stated:

> "There is no such thing as Palestine in [Arab] history, absolutely not."
> According to investigative journalist Joan Peters, who spent seven years researching the origins of the Arab-Jewish conflict over Palestine (From Time Immemorial, 2001), the one identity that was never considered by local inhabitants prior to the 1967 war was "Arab Palestinian."[23]

## The "Mandate" Defined Where Jews Are and Are Not Permitted to Settle

The "Mandate for Palestine" document did not set final borders. It left this for the Mandatory to stipulate in a binding appendix to the final document in the form of a memorandum. However, Article 6 of the "Mandate" clearly states:

> "The Administration of Palestine, while ensuring that the rights and position of other sections of the population are not prejudiced, shall facilitate Jewish immigration under suitable conditions and shall encourage, in co-operation with the Jewish agency referred to in Article 4, close settlement by Jews on the land, including State lands and waste lands not required for public purposes."

Article 25 of the "Mandate for Palestine" entitled the Mandatory to change the terms of the Mandate in the territory east of the Jordan River:

> "In the territories lying between the Jordan and the eastern boundary of Palestine as ultimately determined, the Mandatory shall be entitled, with the consent of the Council of the League of Nations, to postpone or withhold application of such provision of this Mandate as he may consider inapplicable to the existing local conditions ..."

Great Britain activated this option in the above-mentioned memorandum of September 16, 1922, which the Mandatory sent to the League of Nations and which the League subsequently approved—making it a legally binding integral part of the "Mandate."

Thus the "Mandate for Palestine" brought to fruition a fourth Arab state east of the Jordan River, realized in 1946 when the Hashemite Kingdom of Trans-Jordan was granted independence from Great Britain.

All the clauses concerning a Jewish National Home would not apply to this territory [Trans-Jordan] of the original Mandate, as is clearly stated:

> "The following provisions of the Mandate for Palestine are not applicable to the territory known as Trans-Jordan, which comprises all territory lying to the east of a line drawn from ... up the centre of the Wady Araba, Dead Sea and River Jordan. ... His Majesty's Government accept[s] full responsibility as Mandatory for Trans-Jordan."

The creation of an Arab state in eastern Palestine (today Jordan) on 77 percent of the landmass of the original Mandate intended for a Jewish National Home in no way changed the status of Jews west of the Jordan River, nor did it inhibit their right to settle anywhere in western Palestine, the area between the Jordan River and the Mediterranean Sea.

These documents are the last legally binding documents regarding the status of what is commonly called "the West Bank and Gaza."

The September 16, 1922 memorandum is also the last modification of the official terms of the Mandate on record by the League of Nations or by its legal successor—the United Nations—in accordance with Article 27 of the Mandate that states unequivocally:

> "The consent of the Council of the League of Nations is required for any modification of the terms of this mandate."[24]

United Nations Charter recognizes the UN's obligation to uphold the commitments of its predecessor—the League of Nations.[25]

## Political Rights in Palestine Were Granted to Jews Only

The "Mandate for Palestine" clearly differentiates between political rights—referring to Jewish self-determination as an emerging polity—and civil and religious rights, referring to guarantees of equal personal freedoms to non-Jewish residents as individuals and within select communities. Not once are Arabs as a people mentioned in the "Mandate for Palestine." At no point in the entire document is there any granting of political rights to non-Jewish entities (i.e., Arabs). Article 2 of the "Mandate for Palestine" explicitly states that the Mandatory should:

> "... be responsible for placing the country under such political, administrative and economic conditions as will secure the establishment of the Jewish National Home, as laid down in the preamble, and the development of self-governing institutions, and also for safeguarding the civil and religious rights of all the inhabitants of Palestine, irrespective of race and religion."

Political rights to self-determination as a polity for Arabs were guaranteed by the League of Nations in four other mandates – in Lebanon, Syria, Iraq, and later Trans-Jordan [today Jordan].

International law expert Professor Eugene V. Rostow, examining the claim for Arab Palestinian self-determination on the basis of law, concluded:

> "... the mandate implicitly *denies Arab claims* to national political rights in the area *in favor of the Jews*; the mandated territory was in effect reserved to the Jewish people for their self-determination and political development, in acknowledgment of the historic connection of the Jewish people to the land. Lord Curzon, who was then the British Foreign Minister, made this reading of the mandate explicit. There remains simply the theory that the Arab inhabitants of the West Bank and the Gaza Strip have an inherent 'natural law' claim to the area. Neither customary international law nor the United Nations Charter acknowledges that every group of people claiming to be a nation has the right to a state of its own."[26] [italics by author]

## Jewish Peoplehood in Palestine

It is remarkable to note the April 22, 1925 Report of the first High Commissioner on the Administration of Palestine, Sir Herbert Louis Samuel, to the Right Honourable L. S. Amery, M.P., Secretary of State for the Colonies' Government Offices, describing Jewish Peoplehood:

> "During the last two or three generations the Jews have recreated in Palestine a community, now numbering 80,000, of whom about one-fourth are farmers or workers upon the land. This community has its own political organs, an elected assembly for the direction of its domestic concerns, elected councils in the towns, and an organisation for the control of its schools. It has its elected Chief Rabbinate and Rabbinical Council for the direction of its religious affairs. Its business is conducted in Hebrew as a vernacular language, and a Hebrew press serves its needs. It has its distinctive intellectual life and displays considerable economic activity. This community, then, with its town and country population, its political, religious and social organisations, its own language, its own customs, its own life, has in fact *national characteristics*." [italics by author]

## Jerusalem in "Mandate" Time

Two distinct issues exist: the issue of Jerusalem and the issue of the Holy Places. Cambridge Professor Sir Elihu Lauterpacht, Judge ad hoc of the International Court of Justice and a renowned editor of one of the 'bibles' of international law, International Law Reports has said:

> "Not only are the two problems separate; they are also quite distinct in nature from one another. So far as the Holy Places are concerned, the question is for the most part one of assuring respect for the existing interests of the three religions and of providing the necessary guarantees of freedom of access, worship, and religious administration [E.H., as

mandated in Article 13 and 14 of the "Mandate for Palestine"] ... As far as the City of Jerusalem itself is concerned, the question is one of establishing an effective administration of the City which can protect the rights of the various elements of its permanent population—Christian, Arab and Jewish—and ensure the governmental stability and physical security which are essential requirements for the city of the Holy Places."[27]

The notion of internationalizing Jerusalem was never part of the "Mandate":
"Nothing was said in the Mandate about the internationalization of Jerusalem. Indeed Jerusalem as such is not mentioned—though the Holy Places are. And this in itself is a fact of relevance now. For it shows that in 1922 there was no inclination to identify the question of the Holy Places with that of the internationalization of Jerusalem."[28]

Jerusalem the spiritual, political, and historical capital of the Jewish people has served, and still serves, as the political capital of only one nation—the one belonging to the Jewish people.

Jerusalem, a city in Palestine, was and is an undisputed part of the Jewish National Home.

## Jewish Rights to Palestine Were Internationally Guaranteed

In the first Report of the High Commissioner on the Administration of Palestine (1920-1925) presented to the British Secretary of State for the Colonies, published in April 1925, the most senior official of the Mandate, the High Commissioner for Palestine, underscored how international guarantees for the existence of a Jewish National Home in Palestine were achieved:

"The [Balfour] Declaration was endorsed at the time by several of the Allied Governments; it was reaffirmed by the Conference of the Principal Allied Powers at San Remo in 1920; it was subsequently endorsed by unanimous resolutions of both Houses of the Congress of the United States; it was embodied in the Mandate for Palestine approved by the League of Nations in 1922; it was declared, in a formal statement of policy issued by the Colonial Secretary in the same year, 'not to be susceptible of change.' "[29]

Far from the whim of this or that politician or party, eleven successive British governments, Labor and Conservative, from David Lloyd George (1916-1922) through Clement Attlee (1945-1952) viewed themselves as duty-bound to fulfill the "Mandate for Palestine" placed in the hands of Great Britain by the League of Nations.

## United States Government and the "Mandate" Policy

United States President Woodrow Wilson (the twenty-eighth President, 1913-1921) was the founder of the League of Nations for which he was awarded the Nobel Peace Prize in 1919.

Wilson's efforts to join the Unites States as a member of the League of Nations were unsuccessful due to oppositions in the U.S. Senate. Despite not being a member of the League, the U.S. Government claimed on November 20, 1920 that the participation of the United States in WWI entitled it to be consulted as to the terms of the Mandate. The British Government agreed, and the outcome was an agreement calling to safeguard the American interests in Palestine. It concluded with a convention between the United Kingdom and the United States of America, signed on December 3, 1924. It is imperative to note that the convention incorporated the complete text of the "Mandate for Palestine," including the preamble![30]

President Wilson was the first American president to support modern Zionism and Britain's efforts for the creation of a National Home for Jews in Palestine (the text of the Balfour Declaration had been submitted to President Wilson and had been approved by him before its publication).

President Wilson expressed his deep belief in the eventuality of the creation of a Jewish State:

> "I am persuaded," said President Wilson on March 3rd, 1919, "that the Allied nations, with the fullest concurrence of our own Government and people, are agreed that in Palestine shall be laid the foundation of a Jewish Commonwealth."[31]

On June 30, 1922, a joint resolution of both Houses of Congress of the United States unanimously endorsed the "Mandate for Palestine," confirming the irrevocable right of Jews to settle in the area of Palestine—anywhere between the Jordan River and the Mediterranean Sea:

> "Favoring the establishment in Palestine of a national home for the Jewish people.
>
> *"Resolved by the Senate and House of Representatives of the United States of America in Congress assembled.* That the United States of America favors the establishment in Palestine of a national home for the Jewish people, it being clearly understood that nothing shall be done which should prejudice the civil and religious rights of Christian and all other non-Jewish communities in Palestine, and that the holy places and religious buildings and sites in Palestine shall be adequately protected."[32] [italics in the original]

On September 21, 1922, President Warren G. Harding (the twenty-ninth President, 1921-1923) signed the joint resolution of approval to establish a Jewish National Home in Palestine.

## The "Mandate for Palestine" is Valid to This Day

The Mandate survived the demise of the League of Nations. Article 80 of the UN Charter implicitly recognizes the "Mandate for Palestine" of the League of Nations.

This Mandate granted Jews the irrevocable right to settle anywhere in Palestine, the area between the Jordan River and the Mediterranean Sea, a right unaltered in international law and valid to this day. Jewish settlements in Judea and Samaria (i.e. the West Bank), Gaza and the whole of Jerusalem are legal.

The International Court of Justice reaffirmed the meaning and validity of Article 80 in three separate cases:

- ICJ Advisory Opinion of July 11, 1950: in the "question concerning the International States of South West Africa."[33]
- ICJ Advisory Opinion of June 21, 1971: "When the League of Nations was dissolved, the raison d'etre [French: "reason for being"] and original object of these obligations remained. Since their fulfillment did not depend on the existence of the League, they could not be brought to an end merely because the supervisory organ had ceased to exist. ... The International Court of Justice has consistently recognized that the Mandate survived the demise of the League [of Nations]."[34]
- ICJ Advisory Opinion of July 9, 2004: regarding the "legal consequences of the construction of a wall in the occupied Palestinian territory."[35]

In other words, neither the ICJ nor the UN General Assembly can arbitrarily change the status of Jewish settlement as set forth in the "Mandate for Palestine," an international accord that has never been amended.

All of western Palestine, from the Jordan River to the Mediterranean Sea, including the West Bank and Gaza, remains open to Jewish settlement under international law.

Professor Eugene Rostow concurred with the ICJ's opinion as to the "sacredness" of trusts such as the "Mandate for Palestine":

> "'A trust'—as in Article 80 of the UN Charter—does not end because the trustee dies ... the Jewish right of settlement in the whole of western Palestine—the area west of the Jordan—survived the British withdrawal in 1948. ... They are parts of the mandate territory, now legally occupied by Israel with the consent of the Security Council."[36]

The British Mandate left intact the Jewish right to settle in Judea, Samaria and the Gaza Strip. Explains Professor Rostow:

> "This right is protected by Article 80 of the United Nations Charter, which provides that unless a trusteeship agreement is agreed upon (which was not done for the Palestine Mandate), nothing in the chapter shall be construed in and of itself to alter in any manner the rights whatsoever of any states or any peoples or the terms of existing international instruments to which members of the United Nations may respectively be parties.

"The Mandates of the League of Nations have a special status in international law. They are considered to be trusts, indeed 'sacred trusts.'

"Under international law, neither Jordan nor the Palestinian Arab 'people' of the West Bank and the Gaza Strip have a substantial claim to the sovereign possession of the occupied territories."

It is interesting to learn how Article 80 made its way into the UN Charter. Professor Rostow recalls:

"I am indebted to my learned friend Dr. Paul Riebenfeld, who has for many years been my mentor on the history of Zionism, for reminding me of some of the circumstances which led to the adoption of Article 80 of the Charter. Strong Jewish delegations representing differing political tendencies within Jewry attended the San Francisco Conference in 1945. Rabbi Stephen S. Wise, Peter Bergson, Eliahu Elath, Professors Ben-Zion Netanayu and A. S. Yehuda, and Harry Selden were among the Jewish representatives. Their mission was to protect the Jewish right of settlement in Palestine under the mandate against erosion in a world of ambitious states. Article 80 was the result of their efforts."[37]

# Futile Efforts to Challenge the "Mandate for Palestine"

## Myth: The "Mandate for Palestine" is a Class "A" Mandate

There is much to be gained by attributing Class "A" status to the "Mandate for Palestine." If the inhabitants of Palestine were ready for independence under a Class "A" mandate, then the Palestinian Arabs that made up the majority of the inhabitants of Palestine in 1922[38] (589,177 Arabs vs. 83,790 Jews) could logically claim that they were the intended beneficiaries of the "Mandate for Palestine" provided one never reads the actual wording of the document:

1. The "Mandate for Palestine" document *never mentions Class "A" status at any time* for Palestinian Arabs.
2. Article 2 of the document clearly speaks of the Mandatory as being:
   > "... responsible for placing the country under such political, administrative and economic conditions as will secure the establishment of the Jewish national home."

The "Mandate" calls for steps to encourage *Jewish immigration and settlement* throughout Palestine except east of the Jordan River. Historically, therefore, Palestine was an anomaly within the Mandate system, in a class of its own – initially referred to by the British as a "special regime."[39]

Many assume that the "Mandate for Palestine" is a Class "A" Mandate, a common but inaccurate assertion that can be found in many dictionaries and encyclopedias, and is frequently used by the pro-Palestinian media and lately by the ICJ. In the Court Advisory Opinion of July 9, 2004, in the matter of the construction of a wall in the "Occupied Palestinian Territory," the Bench erroneously stated:

> "Palestine was part of the Ottoman Empire. At the end of the First World War, a class [type] 'A' Mandate for Palestine was entrusted to Great Britain by the League of Nations, pursuant to paragraph 4 of Article 22 of the Covenant. ..."[40]

Indeed, Class "A" status was granted to a number of Arab peoples who were ready for independence in the former Ottoman Empire, and only to Arab entities.[41] Palestinian Arabs were not one of these Arab peoples. The Palestine Royal Report clarifies this point:

> "(2) The Mandate [for Palestine] is of a different type from the Mandate for Syria and the Lebanon and the draft Mandate for Iraq. These latter, which were called for convenience "A" Mandates, accorded with the fourth paragraph of Article 22. Thus the Syrian Mandate provided that the government should be based on an organic law which should take into account the rights, interests and wishes of all the inhabitants, and that measures should be enacted 'to facilitate the progressive

development of Syria and the Lebanon as independent States.' The corresponding sentences of the draft Mandate for Iraq were the same. In compliance with them National Legislatures were established in due course on an elective basis.

Article 1 of the Palestine Mandate, on the other hand, vests 'full powers of legislation and of administration,' within the limits of the Mandate, in the Mandatory."[42]

The Palestine Royal Report highlights additional differences between the Mandates:

> "Unquestionably, however, the primary purpose of the Mandate, as expressed in its preamble and its articles, is to promote the establishment of the Jewish National Home.
>
> "... Articles 4, 6 and 11 provide for the recognition of a Jewish Agency 'as a public body for the purpose of advising and co-operating with the Administration' on matters affecting Jewish interests. No such body is envisaged for dealing with Arab interests.[43]
>
> "... But Palestine was different from the other ex-Turkish provinces. It was, indeed, unique both as the Holy Land of three world-religions and as the old historic national home of the Jews. The Arabs had lived in it for centuries, but they had long ceased to rule it, and in view of its peculiar character they could not now claim to possess it in the same way as they could claim possession of Syria or Iraq."[44]

## Myth: The "Mandate" Violates Article 22 of the Covenant of the League of Nations

The Palestinian [British] Royal Commission Report of July 1937 addressed Arab claims that the creation of the Jewish National Home as directed by the "Mandate for Palestine" violated Article 22 of the Covenant of the League of Nations,[45] arguing that they are the communities mentioned in paragraph 4:

> "As to the claim, argued before us by Arab witnesses, that the Palestine Mandate violates Article 22 of the Covenant because it is not in accordance with paragraph 4 thereof, we would point out (a) that the provisional recognition of 'certain communities formerly belonging to the Turkish Empire' as independent nations is permissive; the words are 'can be provisionally recognised,' not 'will' or 'shall': (b) that the penultimate paragraph of Article 22 prescribes that the degree of authority to be exercised by the Mandatory shall be defined, at need, by the Council of the League: (c) that the acceptance by the Allied Powers and the United States of the policy of the Balfour Declaration made it clear from the beginning that Palestine would have to be treated differently from Syria and Iraq, and that this difference of treatment was confirmed by the Supreme Council in the Treaty of Sèvres and by the Council of the League in sanctioning the Mandate.

"This particular question is of less practical importance than it might seem to be. For Article 2 of the Mandate requires 'the development of self-governing institutions'; and, read in the light of the general intention of the Mandate System (of which something will be said presently), this requirement implies, in our judgment, the ultimate establishment of independence.

"(3) The field [Territory] in which the Jewish National Home was to be established was understood, at the time of the Balfour Declaration, to be the whole of historic Palestine, and the Zionists were seriously disappointed when Trans-Jordan was cut away from that field [Territory] under Article 25." [E.H., That excluded 77 percent of historic Palestine—the territory east of the Jordan River, what became later Trans-Jordan].[46]

The Treaty of Sèvres, in Section VII, Articles 94 and 95, makes it clear in each case who are the inhabitants referred to in Paragraph 4 of Article 22 of the Covenant of the League of Nations.

Article 94 distinctly indicates that Paragraph 4 of Article 22 of the Covenant of the League of Nations applies to the Arab inhabitants living within the areas covered by the Mandates for Syria and Mesopotamia. The Article reads:

"The High Contracting Parties agree that Syria and Mesopotamia shall, in accordance with the fourth paragraph of Article 22.

"Part I (Covenant of the League of Nations), be provisionally recognised as independent States subject to the rendering of administrative advice and assistance by a Mandatory until such time as they are able to stand alone..."

Article 95 of the Treaty of Sèvres, however, makes it clear that paragraph 4 of Article 22 of the Covenant of the League of Nations was not to be applied to the Arab inhabitants living within the area to be delineated by the "Mandate for Palestine," but only to the Jews. The Article reads:

"The High Contracting Parties agree to entrust, by application of the provisions of Article 22, the administration of Palestine, within such boundaries as may be determined by the Principal Allied Powers, to a Mandatory to be selected by the said Powers. The Mandatory will be responsible for putting into effect the declaration originally made on November 2, 1917, by the British Government, and adopted by the other Allied Powers, in favour of the establishment in Palestine of a national home for the Jewish people, it being clearly understood that nothing shall be done which may prejudice the civil and religious rights of existing non-Jewish communities in Palestine, or the rights and political status enjoyed by Jews in any other country..."[47]

The second and third paragraphs of the preamble of the "Mandate for Palestine" therefore follow and read:

"Whereas the Principal Allied Powers have also agreed that the Mandatory should be responsible for putting into effect the declaration originally made on November 2, 1917, by the Government of His

Britannic Majesty, and adopted by the said Powers, in favor of the establishment in Palestine of a national home for the Jewish people, it being clearly understood that nothing should be done which might prejudice the civil and religious rights of existing non-Jewish communities in Palestine, or the rights and political status enjoyed by the Jews in any other country; and

"Whereas recognition has thereby been given to the historical connection of the Jewish people with Palestine and to the grounds for reconstituting their national home in that *country*."[48] [italics by author]

Articles 94 and 95 of the Treaty of Sèvres and the "Mandate for Palestine" make it clear:

> The "inhabitants" of the territory for whom the "Mandate for Palestine" was created, who according to the Mandate were "not yet able" to govern themselves and for whom self-determination was a "sacred trust," were not Palestinians, or even Arabs. The "Mandate for Palestine" was created by the predecessor of the United Nations, the League of Nations, *for the Jewish People*.

## Myth: Palestine Was Promised to the Arabs by Sir Henry McMahon

Addressing the Arab claim that Palestine was part of the territories promised to the Arabs in 1915 by Sir Henry McMahon, the British Government stated:

"We think it sufficient for the purposes of this Report to state that the British Government have never accepted the Arab case. When it was first formally presented by the Arab Delegation in London in 1922, the Secretary of State for the Colonies (Mr. Churchill) replied as follows:— 'That letter [Sir H. McMahon's letter of the 24th October, 1915] is quoted as conveying the promise to the Sherif of Mecca to recognize and support the independence of the Arabs within the territories proposed by him. But this promise was given subject to a reservation made in the same letter, which excluded from its scope, among other territories, the portions of Syria lying to the west of the district of Damascus. This reservation has always been regarded by His Majesty's Government as covering the vilayet of Beirut and the independent Sanjak of Jerusalem. The whole of Palestine west of the Jordan was thus excluded from Sir H. McMahon's pledge.'

"It was in the highest degree unfortunate that, in the exigencies of war, the British Government was unable to make their intention clear to the Sherif. Palestine, it will have been noticed, was not expressly mentioned in Sir Henry McMahon's letter of the 24th October, 1915. Nor was any later reference made to it. In the further correspondence between Sir Henry McMahon and the Sherif the only areas relevant to the present discussion which were mentioned were the Vilayets of Aleppo and Beirut. The Sherif asserted that these Vilayets were purely Arab; and, when Sir Henry McMahon pointed out that French interests were involved, he replied that, while he did not recede from his full claims in the north, he did not wish to injure the alliance between Britain and France and would not ask 'for what we now leave to France in Beirut and its coasts' till after the War."[49]

McMahon wrote a letter to The Times [of London] on July 23, 1937, confirming that Palestine was excluded from the area in which Arab independence was promised and that this was well understood by King Hussein.[50]

## Myth: The 1949 "Green Line" is Israel's Internationally Recognized Border

Israel's pre-1967 borders reflected the deployment of Israeli and Arab forces on the ground after Israel's War of Independence in 1948. Professor Judge Stephen M. Schwebel, the former President of the International Court of Justice clarified in his writings "Justice in International Law" that the 1949 armistice demarcation lines are not permanent borders:

> "The armistice agreements of 1949 expressly preserved the territorial claims of all parties and did not purport to establish definitive boundaries between them."[51]

United Nations Security Resolution 54 (July 15, 1948) called upon the Arabs to accept a truce and stop their aggression:

> "*Taking into consideration* that the Provisional Government of Israel has indicated its acceptance in principle of a prolongation of the truce in Palestine; that the States members of the Arab League have rejected successive appeals of the United Nations Mediator, and of the Security Council in its resolution 53 (1948) of 7 July 1948, for the prolongation of the truce in Palestine; and that there has consequently developed a renewal of hostilities in Palestine."[52]

The demarcation line that emerged in the aftermath of the war was drawn up under the auspices of United Nations mediator Dr. Ralph Johnson Bunche. That new boundary largely reflected the ceasefire lines of 1949 and was labeled the "Green Line" merely because a green pencil was used to draw the map of the armistice borders.

## Myth: Palestinian Arabs Seek Peace with Israel

**The PLO Charter**, also known as "the Palestinian National Charter" or "the Palestinian Covenant," was adopted by the Palestine National Council (PNC) on July 1-17, 1968. It reads:

> "**Article 2**: Palestine, with the boundaries it had during the British Mandate, is an indivisible territorial unit.

> "**Article 9**: Armed struggle is the only way to liberate Palestine. Thus it is the overall strategy, not merely a tactical phase. The Palestinian Arab people assert their absolute determination and firm resolution to continue their armed struggle and to work for an armed popular revolution for the liberation of their country and their return to it. They also assert their right to normal life in Palestine and to exercise their right to self-determination and sovereignty over it.

> "**Article 19**: The partition of Palestine in 1947 and the establishment of the state of Israel are entirely illegal, regardless of the passage of time, because they were contrary to the will of the Palestinian people and to their natural right in their homeland, and inconsistent with the principles embodied in the Charter of the United Nations, particularly the right to self-determination.

> "**Article 20**: The Balfour Declaration, the Mandate for Palestine, and everything that has been based upon them, are deemed null and void. Claims of historical or religious ties of Jews with Palestine are incompatible with the facts of history and the true conception of what constitutes statehood. Judaism, being a religion, is not an independent nationality. Nor do Jews constitute a single nation with an identity of its own; they are citizens of the states to which they belong."[53]

**The FATEH Constitution** (referred to, at time, as Fatah) calls under Article 12 for the:

> "Complete liberation of Palestine, and obliteration of Zionist economic, political, military and cultural existence."

As for how it will achieve its goal to wipe Israel off the map, Fateh's constitution, Article 19, minces no words:

> "Armed struggle is a strategy and not a tactic, and the Palestinian Arab People's armed revolution is a decisive factor in the liberation fight and in uprooting the Zionist existence, and this struggle will not cease unless the Zionist state is demolished and Palestine is completely liberated."[54]

**The Hamas Charter** (acronym for "Islamic Resistance Movement" and at time referred to as the Hamas Covenant) states in its second paragraph:[55]

> "Israel will rise and will remain erect until Islam eliminates it as it had eliminated its predecessors. The Martyr, Imam Hassan al-Banna, May Allah Pity his Soul."

# Appendix A – The "Mandate for Palestine"

### LEAGUE OF NATIONS MANDATE FOR PALESTINE (Eretz-Israel)[56]

#### TOGETHER WITH A

### NOTE BY THE SECRETARY-GENERAL RELATING TO ITS APPLICATION

#### TO THE

### TERRITORY KNOWN AS TRANS-JORDAN,
under the provisions of Article 25

*Presented to Parliament by Command of His Majesty, December, 1922.*

### LONDON:
PUBLISHED BY HIS MAJESTY'S STATIONERY OFFICE

## The Council of the League of Nations:

Whereas the Principal Allied Powers have agreed, for the purpose of giving effect to the provisions of Article 22 of the Covenant of the League of Nations, to entrust to a Mandatory selected by the said Powers the administration of the territory of Palestine, which formerly belonged to the Turkish Empire, within such boundaries as may be fixed by them; and

Whereas the Principal Allied Powers have also agreed that the Mandatory should be responsible for putting into effect the declaration originally made on November 2nd, 1917, by the Government of His Britannic Majesty, and adopted by the said Powers, in favor of the establishment in Palestine of a national home for the Jewish people, it being clearly understood that nothing should be done which might prejudice the civil and religious rights of existing non-Jewish communities in Palestine, or the rights and political status enjoyed by Jews in any other country; and

Whereas recognition has thereby been given to the historical connection of the Jewish people with Palestine and to the grounds for reconstituting their national home in that country; and

Whereas the Principal Allied Powers have selected His Britannic Majesty as the Mandatory for Palestine; and

Whereas the mandate in respect of Palestine has been formulated in the following terms and submitted to the Council of the League for approval; and

Whereas His Britannic Majesty has accepted the mandate in respect of Palestine and undertaken to exercise it on behalf of the League of Nations in conformity with the following provisions; and

Whereas by the afore-mentioned Article 22 (paragraph 8), it is provided that the degree of authority, control or administration to be exercised by the Mandatory, not having been previously agreed upon by the Members of the League, shall be explicitly defined by the Council of the League of Nations;

Confirming the said Mandate, defines its terms as follows:

### Article 1.

The Mandatory shall have full powers of legislation and of administration, save as they may be limited by the terms of this mandate.

### Article 2.

The Mandatory shall be responsible for placing the country under such political, administrative and economic conditions as will secure the establishment of the Jewish national home, as laid down in the preamble, and the development of self-governing institutions, and also for safeguarding the civil and religious rights of all the inhabitants of Palestine, irrespective of race and religion.

### Article 3.

The Mandatory shall, so far as circumstances permit, encourage local autonomy.

### Article 4.

An appropriate Jewish agency shall be recognised as a public body for the purpose of advising and co-operating with the Administration of Palestine in such economic, social and other matters as may affect the establishment of the Jewish national home and the interests of the Jewish population in Palestine, and, subject always to the control of the Administration to assist and take part in the development of the country.

The Zionist organization, so long as its organization and constitution are in the opinion of the Mandatory appropriate, shall be recognised as such agency. It shall take steps in consultation with His Britannic Majesty's Government to secure the co-operation of all Jews who are willing to assist in the establishment of the Jewish national home.

### Article 5.

The Mandatory shall be responsible for seeing that no Palestine territory shall be ceded or leased to, or in any way placed under the control of the Government of any foreign Power.

### Article 6.

The Administration of Palestine, while ensuring that the rights and position of other sections of the population are not prejudiced, shall facilitate Jewish immigration under suitable conditions and shall encourage, in co-operation with the Jewish agency referred to in Article 4, close settlement by Jews on the land, including State lands and waste lands not required for public purposes.

### Article 7.

The Administration of Palestine shall be responsible for enacting a nationality law. There shall be included in this law provisions framed so as to facilitate the acquisition of Palestinian citizenship by Jews who take up their permanent residence in Palestine.

### Article 8.

The privileges and immunities of foreigners, including the benefits of consular jurisdiction and protection as formerly enjoyed by Capitulation or usage in the Ottoman Empire, shall not be applicable in Palestine.

Unless the Powers whose nationals enjoyed the afore-mentioned privileges and immunities on August 1, 1914, shall have previously renounced the right to their re-establishment, or shall have agreed to their non-application for a specified period, these privileges and immunities shall, at the expiration of the mandate, be immediately reestablished in their entirety or with such modifications as may have been agreed upon between the Powers concerned.

### Article 9.

The Mandatory shall be responsible for seeing that the judicial system established in Palestine shall assure to foreigners, as well as to natives, a complete guarantee of their rights.

Respect for the personal status of the various peoples and communities and for their religious interests shall be fully guaranteed. In particular, the control and administration of Wakfs shall be exercised in accordance with religious law and the dispositions of the founders.

## Article 10.

Pending the making of special extradition agreements relating to Palestine, the extradition treaties in force between the Mandatory and other foreign Powers shall apply to Palestine.

## Article 11.

The Administration of Palestine shall take all necessary measures to safeguard the interests of the community in connection with the development of the country, and, subject to any international obligations accepted by the Mandatory, shall have full power to provide for public ownership or control of any of the natural resources of the country or of the public works, services and utilities established or to be established therein. It shall introduce a land system appropriate to the needs of the country, having regard, among other things, to the desirability of promoting the close settlement and intensive cultivation of the land.

The Administration may arrange with the Jewish agency mentioned in Article 4 to construct or operate, upon fair and equitable terms, any public works, services and utilities, and to develop any of the natural resources of the country, in so far as these matters are not directly undertaken by the Administration. Any such arrangements shall provide that no profits distributed by such agency, directly or indirectly, shall exceed a reasonable rate of interest on the capital, and any further profits shall be utilised by it for the benefit of the country in a manner approved by the Administration.

## Article 12.

The Mandatory shall be entrusted with the control of the foreign relations of Palestine and the right to issue exequaturs to consuls appointed by foreign Powers. He shall also be entitled to afford diplomatic and consular protection to citizens of Palestine when outside its territorial limits.

## Article 13.

All responsibility in connection with the Holy Places and religious buildings or sites in Palestine, including that of preserving existing rights and of securing free access to the Holy Places, religious buildings and sites and the free exercise of worship, while ensuring the requirements of public order and decorum, is assumed by the Mandatory, who shall be responsible solely to the League of Nations in all matters connected herewith, provided that nothing in this article shall prevent the Mandatory from entering into such arrangements as he may deem reasonable with the Administration for the purpose of carrying the provisions of this article into effect; and provided also that nothing in this mandate shall be construed as conferring upon the Mandatory authority to interfere with the fabric or the management of purely Moslem sacred shrines, the immunities of which are guaranteed.

## Article 14.

A special commission shall be appointed by the Mandatory to study, define and determine the rights and claims in connection with the Holy Places and the rights and claims relating to the different religious communities in Palestine. The method of nomination, the composition and the functions of this Commission shall be submitted to the Council of the League for its approval, and the Commission shall not be appointed or enter upon its functions without the approval of the Council.

### Article 15.

The Mandatory shall see that complete freedom of conscience and the free exercise of all forms of worship, subject only to the maintenance of public order and morals, are ensured to all. No discrimination of any kind shall be made between the inhabitants of Palestine on the ground of race, religion or language. No person shall be excluded from Palestine on the sole ground of his religious belief.

The right of each community to maintain its own schools for the education of its own members in its own language, while conforming to such educational requirements of a general nature as the Administration may impose, shall not be denied or impaired.

### Article 16.

The Mandatory shall be responsible for exercising such supervision over religious or eleemosynary bodies of all faiths in Palestine as may be required for the maintenance of public order and good government. Subject to such supervision, no measures shall be taken in Palestine to obstruct or interfere with the enterprise of such bodies or to discriminate against any representative or member of them on the ground of his religion or nationality.

### Article 17.

The Administration of Palestine may organise on a voluntary basis the forces necessary for the preservation of peace and order, and also for the defence of the country, subject, however, to the supervision of the Mandatory, but shall not use them for purposes other than those above specified save with the consent of the Mandatory. Except for such purposes, no military, naval or air forces shall be raised or maintained by the Administration of Palestine.

Nothing in this article shall preclude the Administration of Palestine from contributing to the cost of the maintenance of the forces of the Mandatory in Palestine.

The Mandatory shall be entitled at all times to use the roads, railways and ports of Palestine for the movement of armed forces and the carriage of fuel and supplies.

### Article 18.

The Mandatory shall see that there is no discrimination in Palestine against the nationals of any State Member of the League of Nations (including companies incorporated under its laws) as compared with those of the Mandatory or of any foreign State in matters concerning taxation, commerce or navigation, the exercise of industries or professions, or in the treatment of merchant vessels or civil aircraft. Similarly, there shall be no discrimination in Palestine against goods originating in or destined for any of the said States, and there shall be freedom of transit under equitable conditions across the mandated area.

Subject as aforesaid and to the other provisions of this mandate, the Administration of Palestine may, on the advice of the Mandatory, impose such taxes and customs duties as it may consider necessary, and take such steps as it may think best to promote the development of the natural resources of the country and to safeguard the interests of the population. It may also, on the advice of the Mandatory, conclude a special customs agreement with any State the territory of which in 1914 was wholly included in Asiatic Turkey or Arabia.

### Article 19.

The Mandatory shall adhere on behalf of the Administration of Palestine to any general international conventions already existing, or which may be concluded hereafter with the approval of the League of Nations, respecting the slave traffic, the traffic in arms and ammunition, or the traffic in drugs, or relating to commercial equality, freedom of transit and navigation, aerial navigation and postal, telegraphic and wireless communication or literary, artistic or industrial property.

### Article 20.

The Mandatory shall co-operate on behalf of the Administration of Palestine, so far as religious, social and other conditions may permit, in the execution of any common policy adopted by the League of Nations for preventing and combating disease, including diseases of plants and animals.

### Article 21.

The Mandatory shall secure the enactment within twelve months from this date, and shall ensure the execution of a Law of Antiquities based on the following rules. This law shall ensure equality of treatment in the matter of excavations and archaeological research to the nationals of all States Members of the League of Nations.

(1)

"Antiquity" means any construction or any product of human activity earlier than the year A. D. 1700.

(2)

The law for the protection of antiquities shall proceed by encouragement rather than by threat.

Any person who, having discovered an antiquity without being furnished with the authorization referred to in paragraph 5, reports the same to an official of the competent Department, shall be rewarded according to the value of the discovery.

(3)

No antiquity may be disposed of except to the competent Department, unless this Department renounces the acquisition of any such antiquity.

No antiquity may leave the country without an export licence from the said Department.

(4)

Any person who maliciously or negligently destroys or damages an antiquity shall be liable to a penalty to be fixed.

(5)

No clearing of ground or digging with the object of finding antiquities shall be permitted, under penalty of fine, except to persons authorised by the competent Department.

(6)

Equitable terms shall be fixed for expropriation, temporary or permanent, of lands which might be of historical or archaeological interest.

(7)

Authorization to excavate shall only be granted to persons who show sufficient guarantees of archaeological experience. The Administration of Palestine shall not, in granting these authorizations, act in such a way as to exclude scholars of any nation without good grounds.

(8)

The proceeds of excavations may be divided between the excavator and the competent Department in a proportion fixed by that Department. If division seems impossible for scientific reasons, the excavator shall receive a fair indemnity in lieu of a part of the find.

### Article 22.

English, Arabic and Hebrew shall be the official languages of Palestine. Any statement or inscription in Arabic on stamps or money in Palestine shall be repeated in Hebrew and any statement or inscription in Hebrew shall be repeated in Arabic.

### Article 23.

The Administration of Palestine shall recognise the holy days of the respective communities in Palestine as legal days of rest for the members of such communities.

### Article 24.

The Mandatory shall make to the Council of the League of Nations an annual report to the satisfaction of the Council as to the measures taken during the year to carry out the provisions of the mandate. Copies of all laws and regulations promulgated or issued during the year shall be communicated with the report.

### Article 25.

In the territories lying between the Jordan and the eastern boundary of Palestine as ultimately determined, the Mandatory shall be entitled, with the consent of the Council of the League of Nations, to postpone or withhold application of such provisions of this mandate as he may consider inapplicable to the existing local conditions, and to make such provision for the administration of the territories as he may consider suitable to those conditions, provided that no action shall be taken which is inconsistent with the provisions of Articles 15, 16 and 18.

### Article 26.

The Mandatory agrees that, if any dispute whatever should arise between the Mandatory and another member of the League of Nations relating to the interpretation or the application of the provisions of the mandate, such dispute, if it cannot be settled by negotiation, shall be submitted to the Permanent Court of International Justice provided for by Article 14 of the Covenant of the League of Nations.

**Article 27.**

The consent of the Council of the League of Nations is required for any modification of the terms of this mandate.

**Article 28.**

In the event of the termination of the mandate hereby conferred upon the Mandatory, the Council of the League of Nations shall make such arrangements as may be deemed necessary for safeguarding in perpetuity, under guarantee of the League, the rights secured by Articles 13 and 14, and shall use its influence for securing, under the guarantee of the League, that the Government of Palestine will fully honour the financial obligations legitimately incurred by the Administration of Palestine during the period of the mandate, including the rights of public servants to pensions or gratuities.

The present instrument shall be deposited in original in the archives of the League of Nations and certified copies shall be forwarded by the Secretary-General of the League of Nations to all members of the League.

Done at London the twenty-fourth day of July, one thousand nine hundred and twenty-two.

*Certified true copy:*

**FOR THE SECRETARY-GENERAL,**

**RAPPARD,**

*Director of the Mandates Section.*

# Appendix B—Article 25 of the "Mandate" Was Realized

Geneva, September 23, 1922
Territory known as Trans-Jordan

## Note by the Secretary-General

The Secretary-General has the honour to communicate for the information of the Members of the League, a memorandum relating to Article 25 of the Palestine Mandate presented by the British Government to the Council of the League on September 16th, 1922.

The memorandum was approved by the Council subject to the decision taken at its meeting in London on July 24th, 1922, with regard to the coming into force of the Palestine and Syrian mandates.

## Memorandum by the British Representative

1. Article 25 of the Mandate for Palestine provides as follows:
> "In the territories lying between the Jordan and the eastern boundary of Palestine as ultimately determined, the Mandatory shall be entitled, with the consent of the Council of the League of Nations, to postpone or withhold application of such provision of this Mandate as he may consider inapplicable to the existing local conditions, and to make such provision for the administration of the territories as he may consider suitable to those conditions, provided no action shall be taken which is inconsistent with the provisions of Articles 15, 16 and 18."

2. In pursuance of the provisions of this Article, His Majesty's Government invite the Council to pass the following resolution:
> "The following provisions of the Mandate for Palestine are not applicable to the territory known as Trans-Jordan, which comprises all territory lying to the east of a line drawn from a point two miles west of the town of Akaba on the Gulf of that name up the centre of the Wady Araba, Dead Sea and River Jordan to its junction with the River Yarmuk; thence up the centre of that river to the Syrian Frontier."

*Preamble.* - Recitals 2 and 3.

Article 2. - The words "placing the country under such political administration and economic conditions as will secure the establishment of the Jewish national home, as laid down in the preamble, and."

Article 4.

Article 6.

Article 7. - The sentence "The shall be included in this law provisions framed so as to facilitate the acquisition of Palestinian citizenship by Jews who take up their permanent residence in Palestine."

Article 11. - The second sentence of the first paragraph and the second paragraph.

Article 13.

Article 14.

Article 22.

Article 23.

In the application of the Mandate to Trans-Jordan, the action which, in Palestine, is taken by the Administration of the latter country, will be taken by the Administration of Trans-Jordan under the general supervision of the Mandatory.

3. His Majesty's Government accept full responsibility as Mandatory for Trans-Jordan, and undertake that such provision as may be made for the administration of that territory in accordance with Article 25 of the Mandate shall be in no way inconsistent with those provisions of the Mandate which are not by this resolution declared inapplicable.

# Appendix C – Article 22 of the Covenant of the League of Nations[57]

June 28, 1919

1. To those colonies and territories which as a consequence of the late war have ceased to be under the sovereignty of the States which formerly governed them and which are inhabited by peoples not yet able to stand by themselves under the strenuous conditions of the modern world, there should be applied the principle that the well-being and development of such peoples form a sacred trust of civilization and that securities for the performance of this trust should be embodied in this Covenant.
2. The best method of giving practical effect to this principle is that the tutelage of such peoples should be entrusted to advanced nations who by reason of their resources, their experience or their geographical position can best undertake this responsibility, and who are willing to accept it, and that this tutelage should be exercised by them as Mandatories on behalf of the League.
3. The character of the mandate must differ according to the stage of the development of the people, the geographical situation of the territory, its economic condition and other similar circumstances.
4. Certain communities formerly belonging to the Turkish Empire have reached a stage of development where their existence as independent nations can be provisionally recognized, subject to the rendering of administrative advice and assistance by a Mandatory until such time as they are able to stand alone. The wishes of these communities must be a principal consideration in the selection of the Mandatory.
5. Other peoples, especially those of Central Africa, are at such a stage that the Mandatory must be responsible for the administration of the territory under conditions which will guarantee freedom of conscience and religion, subject only to the maintenance of public order and morals, the prohibition of abuses such as the slave trade, the arms traffic and the liquor traffic, and the prevention of the establishment of fortifications or military and naval bases and of military training of the natives for other than police purposes and the defence of territory, and will also secure equal opportunities for the trade and commerce of other Members of the League.
6. There are territories, such as South West Africa and certain of the South Pacific Islands, which, owing to the sparseness of their population, or their small size, or their remoteness from the centres of civilization, or their geographical contiguity to the territory of the Mandatory, and other circumstances, can be best administered under the laws of the Mandatory as integral portions of its territory, subject to the safeguards above mentioned in the interests of the indigenous population.

7. In every case of mandate, the Mandatory shall render to the Council an annual report in reference to the territory committed to its charge.
8. The degree of authority, control, or administration to be exercised by the Mandatory shall, if not previously agreed upon by the Members of the League, be explicitly defined in each case by the Council.
9. A permanent Commission shall be constituted to receive and examine the annual reports of the Mandatories and to advise the Council on all matters relating to the observance of the mandates.

# Appendix D – UN Resolution 181 Recommendation to Partition Palestine

In 1947 the British put the future of western Palestine into the hands of the United Nations, the successor organization to the League of Nations which had established the Mandate for Palestine. A UN Commission recommended partitioning what was left of the original Mandate—western Palestine—into two new states, one Jewish and one Arab.[58] Jerusalem and its surrounding villages were to be temporarily classified as an international zone belonging to neither polity.

Resolution 181 was a none-binding *recommendation to partition Palestine*, whose implementation hinged on acceptance by both parties—Arabs and Jews. The resolution was adopted on November 29, 1947 in the General Assembly by a vote of 33 to 12, with 10 abstentions. Among the supporters were both the United States and the Soviet Union, and other nations including France and Australia. The Arab nations, including Egypt, Syria, Iraq, and Saudi Arabia denounced the plan on the General Assembly floor and voted as a bloc against Resolution 181 *promising* to defy its implementation *by force*. [italics by author]

The resolution recognized the need for immediate Jewish statehood (and a parallel Arab state), but the 'blueprint' for peace became a moot issue when the Arabs refused to accept it. Subsequently, realities on the ground in the wake of Arab aggression (and Israel's survival) became the basis for UN efforts to bring peace. Resolution 181 lost its validity and relevance.

Aware of Arabs' past aggression, Resolution 181, in paragraph C, calls on the Security Council to:

> "… determine as a threat to the peace, breach of the peace or *act of aggression*, in accordance with Article 39 of the Charter, any attempt to *alter by force* the settlement envisaged by this resolution." [italics by author]

The ones who sought to alter by force the settlement envisioned in Resolution 181 were the Arabs who threatened *bloodshed* if the UN were to adopt the Resolution:

> "The [British] Government of Palestine fear that strife in Palestine will be greatly intensified when the Mandate is terminated, and that the international status of the United Nations Commission will mean little or nothing to the Arabs in Palestine, to whom *the killing of Jews now transcends all other considerations*. Thus, the Commission will be faced with the problem of how to avert certain *bloodshed* on a very much wider scale than prevails at present. … The Arabs have made it quite clear and have told the Palestine government that they do not propose to co-operate or to assist the Commission, and that, far from it, they *propose to attack and impede* its work in every possible way. We have no reason to suppose that they do not mean what they say."[59] [italics by author]

## Map: The Recommendation to Partition Palestine

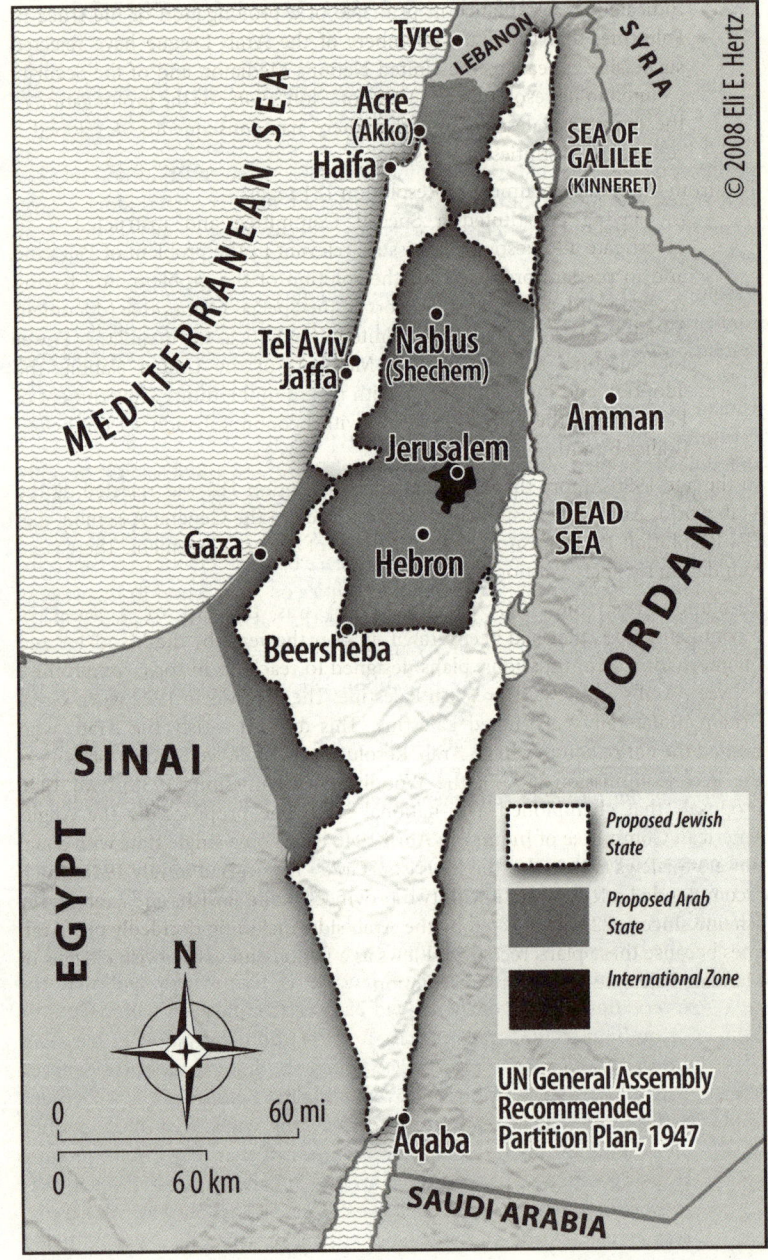

Arabs' intentions and deeds did not fare better after Resolution 181 was adopted:
"Taking into consideration that the Provisional Government of Israel has indicated its acceptance in principle of a prolongation of the truce in Palestine; that the States members of the Arab League have rejected successive appeals of the United Nations Mediator, and of the Security Council in its resolution 53 (1948) of 7 July 1948, for the prolongation of the truce in Palestine; and that there has consequently developed a renewal of hostilities in Palestine."

Text from the actual document of Resolution 181 reads:
"... Having constituted a Special Committee and instructed it to investigate all questions and issues relevant to the problem of Palestine, and to prepare proposals for the solution of the problem, and having received and examined the report of the Special Committee (document A/364). ... *Recommends* to the United Kingdom, as the mandatory Power for Palestine, and to all other Members of the United Nations the adoption and implementation, with regard to the future Government of Palestine, of the Plan of Partition with Economic Union set out below."
[italics by author]

In the late 1990s, more than 50 years after Resolution 181 was rejected by the Arab world, Arab leaders suddenly recommended to the General Assembly that UN Resolution 181 be resurrected as the basis of a peace agreement. There is no foundation for such a notion.

Resolution 181 (the 1947 Partition Plan) was the last of a series of recommendations that had been drawn up over the years by the Mandator and by international commissions, plans designed to reach an historic compromise between Arabs and Jews in western Palestine. The first was in 1922 when Great Britain unilaterally partitioned Palestine. This did not satisfy the Arabs who wanted the entire country to be Arab. Resolution 181 followed such proposals as the Peel Commission (1937); the Woodhead Commission (1938); two 1946 proposals that championed a bi-national state; one proposed by the Anglo-American Committee of Inquiry in April 1946 based on a single state with equal powers for Jews and Arabs; the Morrison-Grady Plan raised in July 1946 which recommended a federal state with two provinces – one Jewish, one Arab. Every scheme since 1922 was rejected by the Arab side, including decidedly pro-Arab ones because these plans recognized Jews as a nation and gave Jewish citizens of Mandate Palestine political representation.

## Position of the Representative of the Jewish-Agency

In a statement by the representative of the Jewish Agency for Palestine, Dr. Abba Hillel Silver, in October 1947 before the United Nations Special Committee on Palestine (UNSCOP), had this to say about fairness, balance, and justice:[60]

> "According to David Lloyd George, then British Prime Minister, the Balfour Declaration implied that the whole of Palestine, including Transjordan, should ultimately become a Jewish state. Transjordan had, nevertheless, been severed from Palestine in 1922 and had subsequently been set up as an Arab kingdom. Now a second Arab state was to be carved out of the remainder of Palestine, with the result that the Jewish National Home would represent less than one eighth of the territory originally set aside for it. Such a sacrifice should not be asked of the Jewish people."

Referring to the Arab States established as independent countries since the First World War, he said:

> "17,000,000 Arabs now occupied an area of 1,290,000 square miles, including all the principal Arab and Moslem centres, while Palestine, after the loss of Transjordan, was only 10,000 square miles; yet the majority plan proposed to reduce it by one half. UNSCOP proposed to eliminate Western Galilee from the Jewish State; that was an injustice and a grievous handicap to the development of the *Jewish State*."[61] [italics by author]

## Israel's Independence is Not a Result of a Partial Implementation of the Partition Plan

Resolution 181 has no legal ramifications—that is, Resolution 181 recognized the Jewish right to statehood, but its validity as a potentially legal and binding document was never consummated. Like the schemes that preceded it, Resolution 181's validity hinged on acceptance by both parties of the General Assembly's *recommendation*.

Cambridge Professor Sir Elihu Lauterpacht, Judge ad hoc of the International Court of Justice and a renowned expert on international law, clarified that from a legal standpoint, the 1947 UN Partition Resolution had no legislative character to vest territorial rights in either Jews or Arabs. In a monograph relating to one of the most complex aspects of the territorial issue, the status of Jerusalem, Judge, Sir Lauterpacht wrote that any binding force the Partition Plan would have had to arise from the principle *pacta sunt servanda* [Latin: "Treaties must be honored"], the first principle of international law, that is, from agreement of the parties at variance to the proposed plan. In the case of Israel, Judge, Sir Lauterpacht explains:

> "... the coming into existence of Israel does not depend legally upon the Resolution. The right of a State to exist flows from its factual existence, especially when that existence is prolonged, shows every sign of continuance and is recognised by the generality of nations."[62]

Reviewing Lauterpacht's arguments, Professor Stone, a distinguished authority on the Law of Nations, added that Israel's "legitimacy" or the "legal foundation" for its birth does not reside with the United Nations' Partition Plan, which as a consequence of Arab actions became a dead issue. Professor Stone concluded:

> "... The State of Israel is thus not legally derived from the partition plan, but rests (as do most other states in the world) on assertion of independence by its people and government, on the vindication of that independence by arms against assault by other states, and on the establishment of orderly government within territory under its stable control."[63]

## Arab's Aggression Before and After the Adoption of Resolution 181

Following passage of Resolution 181 by the General Assembly, Arab countries took the dais to reiterate their absolute rejection of the recommendation and intention to render implementation of Resolution 181 a moot question by the use of force. These examples from the transcript of the General Assembly plenary meeting on November 29, 1947 speak for themselves:

> "Mr. JAMALI (Iraq): ... We believe that the decision which we have now taken ... undermines peace, justice and democracy. In the name of my Government, I wish to state that it feels that this decision is antidemocratic, illegal, impractical and contrary to the Charter ... Therefore, in the name of my Government, I wish to put on record that Iraq does not recognize the validity of this decision, will reserve freedom of action towards its implementation, and holds those who were influential in passing it against the free conscience of mankind responsible for the consequences."

> "Amir. ARSLAN (Syria): ... Gentlemen, the Charter is dead. But it did not die a natural death; it was murdered, and you all know who is guilty. My country will never recognize such a decision [Partition]. It will never agree to be responsible for it. Let the consequences be on the heads of others, not on ours."

> "H. R. H. Prince Seif El ISLAM ABDULLAH (Yemen): The Yemen delegation has stated previously that the partition plan is contrary to justice and to the Charter of the United Nations. Therefore, the Government of Yemen does not consider itself bound by such a decision ... and will reserve its freedom of action towards the implementation of this decision."[64]

The Partition Plan was met not only by verbal rejection on the Arab side but also by concrete, bellicose steps to block its implementation and destroy the Jewish polity by force of arms, a goal the Arabs publicly declared even before Resolution 181 was brought to a vote.

Arabs not only rejected the compromise and took action to prevent establishment of a Jewish state but also blocked establishment of an Arab state under the partition plan not just *before* the Israel War of Independence, but also *after* the war when they themselves controlled the West Bank (1948-1967), rendering the *recommendation* 'a still birth.'

The UN itself recognized that 181 had not been accepted by the Arab side, rendering it a dead issue: On January 29, 1948, the First Monthly Progress Report of the UN-appointed Palestine Commission, charged with helping put Resolution 181 into effect was submitted to the Security Council (A/AC.21/7). Implementation of Resolution 181 hinged not only on the five Member States appointed to represent the UN (Bolivia, Czechoslovakia, Denmark, Panama, Philippines) and Great Britain, but first and foremost on the participation of the *two sides* who were invited to appoint representatives. The Commission then reported:

> "The invitation extended by the [181] resolution was promptly accepted by the Government of the United Kingdom and by the Jewish Agency for Palestine, both of which designated representatives to assist the commission. ... As regards the Arab Higher Committee, the following telegraphic response was received by the Secretary-General on 19 January:
>
> ARAB HIGHER COMMITTEE IS DETERMINED PRESIST [PERSIST] IN REJECTION PARTITION AND IN REFUSAL RECOGNIZE UN[O] RESOLUTION THIS RESPECT AND ANYTHING DERIVING THEREFROM [THERE FROM]. FOR THESE REASONS IT IS UNABLE [TO] ACCEPT [THE] INVITATION."[65]

The UN Palestine Commission's February 16, 1948 report (A/AC.21/9) to the Security Council noted that Arab-led hostilities were an effort:

> "to prevent the implementation of the [General] Assembly's plan of partition, and to thwart its objectives by threats and acts of violence, including armed incursions into Palestinian territory."

On May 17, 1948—after the invasion into Israel began—the Palestine Commission designed to implement 181 adjourned sine die [Latin: "without determining a future date"], after the General Assembly appointed a United Nations Mediator in Palestine, which relieved the United Nations Palestine Commission from the further exercise of its responsibilities.

At the time, some thought the Partition Plan could be revived, but by the end of the war Resolution 181 had become a moot issue as realities on the ground made establishment of an armistice-line [the "Green Line"]—a temporary ceasefire line expected to be followed by peace treaties—the most constructive path to solving the conflict.

A July 30, 1949 working paper of the UN Secretariat entitled The Future of Arab Palestine and the Question of Partition noted further that:

> "The Arabs rejected the United Nations Partition Plan so that any comment of theirs did not specifically concern the status of the Arab section of Palestine under partition but rather rejected the scheme in its entirety."[66]

By the time armistice agreements were reached in 1949 between Israel and its immediate Arab neighbors (Egypt, Lebanon, Syria and Jordan) with the assistance of UN mediator Dr. Ralph Bunche—Resolution 181 had become irrelevant, and the armistice agreements addressed new realities created by the war. Over subsequent years, the UN simply abandoned the recommendations contained in Resolution 181, as its ideas were drained of all relevance by events. Moreover, the Arabs continued to reject 181 *after* the war when they themselves controlled the West Bank (1948-1967) which Jordan invaded in the course of the war and annexed illegally.

Attempts by Palestinians in the past decade (and recently by the ICJ) to 'roll back the clock' and resuscitate Resolution 181 more than five decades after they rejected it 'as if nothing had happened' are a baseless ploy designed to use Resolution 181 as leverage to bring about a greater Israeli withdrawal from parts of western Palestine and to gain a broader base from which to continue to attack Israel with even less defendable borders. Both Palestinians and their Arab brethren in neighboring countries rendered the plan null and void by their own subsequent aggressive actions.

Professor Stone wrote about this 'novelty of resurrection' in 1981 when he analyzed a similar attempt by pro-Palestinian 'experts' at the UN to rewrite the history of the conflict. Their writings were termed "Studies," Stone called it "revival of the dead"

> "To attempt to show ... that Resolution 181 (II) 'remains' in force in 1981 is thus an undertaking even more *miraculous* than would be the *revival of the dead*. It is an attempt to give life to an entity that the Arab states had themselves aborted before it came to maturity and birth. To propose that Resolution 181 (II) can be treated as if it has binding force in 1981, [E.H., the year the book was written] for the benefit of the same Arab states, who by their aggression destroyed it *ab initio* [In Latin: "From the beginning"], also violates 'general principles of law,' such as those requiring claimants to equity to come 'with clean hands,' and forbidding a party who has unlawfully repudiated a transaction from holding the other party to terms that suit the later expediencies of the repudiating party." [italics by author]

Resolution 181 had been tossed into the waste bin of history, along with the Partition Plans that preceded it.

# Appendix E – Israel's Declaration of Independence

**Provisional Government of Israel**
*Official Gazette*: Number 1; Tel Aviv, 5 Iyar 5708, 14.5.1948 Page 1

## Declaration of the Establishment of the State of Israel

The Land of Israel was the birthplace of the Jewish people. Here their spiritual, religious and political identity was shaped. Here they first attained to statehood, created cultural values of national and universal significance and gave to the world the eternal Book of Books.

After being forcibly exiled from their land, the people kept faith with it throughout their Dispersion and never ceased to pray and hope for their return to it and for the restoration in it of their political freedom.

Impelled by this historic and traditional attachment, Jews strove in every successive generation to re-establish themselves in their ancient homeland. In recent decades they returned in their masses. Pioneers, defiant returnees, and defenders, they made deserts bloom, revived the Hebrew language, built villages and towns, and created a thriving community controlling its own economy and culture, loving peace but knowing how to defend itself, bringing the blessings of progress to all the country's inhabitants, and aspiring towards independent nationhood.

> In the year 5657 (1897), at the summons of the spiritual father of the Jewish State, Theodore Herzl, the First Zionist Congress convened and proclaimed the right of the Jewish people to national rebirth in its own country.
>
> This right was recognized in the Balfour Declaration of the 2nd November, 1917, and re-affirmed in the Mandate of the League of Nations which, in particular, gave international sanction to the historic connection between the Jewish people and Eretz-Israel and to the right of the Jewish people to rebuild its National Home.

The catastrophe which recently befell the Jewish people—the massacre of millions of Jews in Europe—was another clear demonstration of the urgency of solving the problem of its homelessness by re-establishing in Eretz-Israel the Jewish State, which would open the gates of the homeland wide to every Jew and confer upon the Jewish people the status of a fully privileged member of the community of nations.

Survivors of the Nazi holocaust in Europe, as well as Jews from other parts of the world, continued to migrate to *Eretz-Israel*, undaunted by difficulties, restrictions and dangers, and never ceased to assert their right to a life of dignity, freedom and honest toil in their national homeland.

In the Second World War, the Jewish community of this country contributed its full share to the struggle of the freedom- and peace-loving nations against the forces of Nazi wickedness and, by the blood of its soldiers and its war effort, gained the right to be reckoned among the peoples who founded the United Nations.

On the 29th November, 1947, the United Nations General Assembly passed a resolution calling for the establishment of a Jewish State in *Eretz-Israel*; the General Assembly required the inhabitants of *Eretz-Israel* to take such steps as were necessary on their part for the implementation of that resolution. This recognition by the United Nations of the right of the Jewish people to establish their State is irrevocable.

This right is the natural right of the Jewish people to be masters of their own fate, like all other nations, in their own sovereign State.

Accordingly we, members of the People's Council, representatives of the Jewish Community of *Eretz-Israel* and of the Zionist Movement, are here assembled on the day of the termination of the British Mandate over *Eretz-Israel* and, by virtue of our natural and historic right and on the strength of the resolution of the United Nations General Assembly, hereby declare the establishment of a Jewish state in *Eretz-Israel*, to be known as the State of Israel.

We declare that, with effect from the moment of the termination of the Mandate being tonight, the eve of Sabbath, the 6th Iyar, 5708 (15th May, 1948), until the establishment of the elected, regular authorities of the State in accordance with the Constitution which shall be adopted by the Elected Constituent Assembly not later than the 1st October 1948, the People's Council shall act as a Provisional Council of State, and its executive organ, the People's Administration, shall be the Provisional Government of the Jewish State, to be called "Israel."

The State of Israel will be open for Jewish immigration and for the Ingathering of the Exiles; it will foster the development of the country for the benefit of all its inhabitants; it will be based on freedom, justice and peace as envisaged by the prophets of Israel; it will ensure complete equality of social and political rights to all its inhabitants irrespective of religion, race or sex; it will guarantee freedom of religion, conscience, language, education and culture; it will safeguard the Holy Places of all religions; and it will be faithful to the principles of the Charter of the United Nations.

The State of Israel is prepared to cooperate with the agencies and representatives of the United Nations in implementing the resolution of the General Assembly of the 29th November, 1947, and will take steps to bring about the economic union of the whole of *Eretz-Israel*.

We appeal to the United Nations to assist the Jewish people in the building-up of its State and to receive the State of Israel into the community of nations.

We appeal—in the very midst of the onslaught launched against us now for months—to the Arab inhabitants of the State of Israel to preserve peace and participate in the upbuilding of the State on the basis of full and equal citizenship and due representation in all its provisional and permanent institutions.

We extend our hand to all neighboring states and their peoples in an offer of peace and good neighborliness, and appeal to them to establish bonds of cooperation and mutual help with the sovereign Jewish people settled in its own land. The State of Israel is prepared to do its share in a common effort for the advancement of the entire Middle East.

We appeal to the Jewish people throughout the Diaspora to rally round the Jews of Eretz-Israel in the tasks of immigration and upbuilding and to stand by them in the great struggle for the realization of the age-old dream—the redemption of Israel.

Placing our trust in the Almighty, we affix our signatures to this proclamation at this session of the provisional Council of State, on the soil of the Homeland, in the city of Tel-Aviv, on this Sabbath eve, the 5th day of Iyar, 5708 (14th May, 1948).

**Signatories:**

David Ben-Gurion, Daniel Auster, Mordekhai Bentov, Yitzchak Ben Zvi, Eliyahu Berligne, Fritz Bernstein, Rabbi Wolf Gold, Meir Grabovsky, Yitzchak Gruenbaum, Dr. Abraham Granovsky, Eliyahu Dobkin, Meir Wilner-Kovner, Zerach Wahrhaftig, Herzl Vardi, Rachel Cohen, Rabbi Kalman Kahana, Saadia Kobashi, Rabbi Yitzchak Meir Levin, Meir David Loewenstein, Zvi Luria, Golda Myerson, Nachum Nir, Zvi Segal, Rabbi Yehuda Leib Hacohen Fishman, David Zvi Pinkas, Aharon Zisling Moshe Kolodny, Eliezer Kaplan, Abraham Katznelson, Felix Rosenblueth, David Remez, Berl Repetur, Mordekhai Shattner, Ben Zion Sternberg, Bekhor Shitreet, Moshe Shapira, Moshe Shertok.

## "Redemption of Palestine ..."

" ... [The Jews] are much more than hewers of wood and drawers of water; they read, they think, they discuss; in the evenings they have music, classes, lectures; there is among them a real activity of mind. And the-third factor is that they are fully conscious that they are not engaged in some casual task, without special significance other than the provision of their own livelihood; they know quite well that they are an integral part of the movement for the *redemption of Palestine*; that they, few though they may be, are the representatives, and in a sense the agents, of the whole of Jewry; that the daily work in which they are engaged is in touch with the prophecies of old and with the prayers of millions now. So they find the labour of their hands to be worthy in itself; it is made lighter by intellectual activity; it is ennobled by the patriotic ideal which it serves. That is the reason why these pioneers are happy." [italics by author]

The High Commissioner
Administration of Palestine
Jerusalem, 22 April, 1925

# Appendix F – Israel's Government Position

**Yehuda Z. Blum, Ambassador and Permanent Representative of Israel to the United Nations. At the Louis D. Brandeis Award Dinner of the Zionist Organization of America. (Washington D.C., 11 June 1979)**[67]

"A corollary of the inalienable right of the Jewish people to its Land is the right to live in any part of Eretz Yisrael, including Judea and Samaria which are an integral part of Eretz Yisrael. Jews are not foreigners anywhere in the Land of Israel. Anyone who asserts that it is illegal for a Jew to live in Judea and Samaria just because he is a Jew, is in fact advocating a concept that is disturbingly reminiscent of the 'Judenrein' policies of Nazi Germany banning Jews from certain spheres of life for no other reason than that they were Jews. The Jewish villages in Judea, Samaria and the Gaza district are there as of right and are there to stay.

"The right of Jews to settle in the Land of Israel was also recognised in the League of Nations 'Mandate for Palestine' which stressed 'the historical connection of the Jewish people with Palestine and … the grounds for reconstituting' - I repeat, reconstituting 'their national home in that country.'

"The Mandatory Power was also entrusted with the duty to encourage 'close settlement by Jews on the land, including state lands and waste lands not required for public purposes.'"

## Notes:

This document uses extensive links via the Internet. If you experience a broken link, please note the 5-digit number (xxxxx) at the end of the URL and use it as a Keyword in the Search Box at: **www.MEfacts.com**.

1. *The Jewish State* by Theodor Herzl, 1896. Translated from German by Sylvie D'Avigdor. This edition was published in 1946 by the American Zionist Emergency Council.
2. The British Foreign Office, November 2, 1917.
3. "The total land area of Palestine is estimated at 26,320 square kms. or 10,162 square miles. In addition there is an inland water area of 704 square kms. or 272 square miles, comprising Lake Huleh, Lake Tiberias and one half of the Dead Sea. The total area of the country is thus 27,024 square kms. or 10,434 square miles." See "A Survey of Palestine" Volume I. Chapter III, p. 103. Prepared December 1945-January 1946 for the Anglo-American Committee of Inquiry.
4. The 51 member countries of the League of Nations as of July 24, 1922: Albania, Argentina, Australia, Austria, Belgium, Bolivia, Brazil, British India, Bulgaria, Canada, Chile, Colombia, Costa Rica, Cuba, Czechoslovakia, Denmark, El Salvador, Estonia, Finland, France, Greece, Guatemala, Haiti, Honduras, Italy, Japan, Kingdom of Serbs, Croats, and Slovenes, Latvia, Liberia, Lithuania, Luxembourg, Netherlands, New Zealand, Nicaragua, Norway, Panama, Paraguay, Persia, Peru, Poland, Portugal, Republic of China, Romania, Siam, Spain, Sweden, Switzerland, Union of South Africa, United Kingdom, Uruguay, and Venezuela.
5. Minutes of Meeting of Council, Geneva, September 29, 1923. (11923)
6. See the preamble to the "Mandate for Palestine."
7. See introductory chapter to Bernard Lewis, *The Crisis in Islam: Holy War and Unholy Terror* (New York: Modern Library, 2003.)
8. For a discussion of this characteristic, which has stymied attempts to create genuine nationhood and transformed anti-Zionism into unifying factor around which Arab nationalism could be crystallized, see Avi Shlaim's review of Adeed Dawisha's Arab Nationalism in the 20th Century: *From Triumph to Despair*, reviewed in *The Guardian*, March 29,2003. See: http://education.guardian.co.uk/higher/books/story/0,10595,924043,00.html. (10818)
9. This insight was raised in a July 11, 2003 op-ed piece in the Hebrew daily *Yedioth Aharonoth*.
10. See Article 2 of the "Mandate for Palestine."
11. See "Introductory," Page 1 of the Report by the Majesty's Government in the United Kingdom of Great Britain and Northern Ireland to the Council of the League of Nations on the Administration of Palestine and Trans-Jordan for the year 1938.
12. For more on this subject, see Popular Searches: Territories and Palestinians, at: www.mefacts.com.

13. Until recently, no Arab nation or group recognized or claimed the existence of an independent Palestinian nationality or ethnicity. Arabs who happened to live in Palestine denied that they had a unique Palestinian identity. The First Congress of Muslim-Christian Associations (Jerusalem, February 1919) met to select Palestinian Arab representatives for the Paris Peace Conference. They adopted the following resolution: "We consider Palestine as part of Arab Syria, as it has never been separated from it at any time. We are connected with it by national, religious, linguistic, natural, economic and geographical bonds." See Yehoshua Porath, *The Palestinian Arab National Movement: From Riots to Rebellion* (London: Frank Cass and Co., Ltd., 1977) vol. 2, pp. 81-82.

14. For a Christian perspective of the "Palestinian people" myth, see *The Jewish Roots of Christianity—The Myth of Palestine* at: www.rbooker.com/html/the_myth_of_palestine.html. (11500)

15. See the 1st Congress of Muslim-Christian Associations to the Paris Peace Conference, Jerusalem, February 1919. For an in-depth article on Palestinians' Syrian identity, see Daniel Pipes, *Palestine for the Syrians?*, Commentary (December 1986) at: www.danielpipes.org/pf.php?id=174. (11501)

16. Document's text can be found in the Yale University online law library. British documents, such as the White Paper of 1939, speak of "Jews and Arabs" or "the Arabs of Palestine," and even the United Nations 1947 Partition Plan speaks of "Arab and Jewish states." There were no "Palestinians." See: www.yale.edu/lawweb/avalon/mideast/mideast.htm. (11587)

17. Mentioned in the report by the High Commissioner on the Administration of Palestine 1920-1925 to the Right Honorable L. S. Amery, M.P. Secretary of State for the Colonies. Government Offices, Jerusalem, April 22, 1925.

18. "Dear pupil, do you know who the Palestinians are? The Palestinian people are descended from the Canaanites." See the survey and quotes from Palestinian textbooks at: www.edume.org. (11503)

19. For information on the coining of the name Palestine and Philistine origins, see Rockwell Lazareth, *Who are the Palestinians? What and Where is Palestine?* at: www.newswithviews.com/israel/israel14.htm. (11504)

20. See Daniel Pipes, *Greater Syria: History of an Ambition* (Oxford: Oxford University Press, 1990) at: www.danielpipes.org/books/greaterchap.shtml. (11498)

21. "Political History & System of Government—Jordan's State Building and the Palestinian Problem," Embassy of the Hashemite Kingdom of Jordan, at: www.jordanembassyus.org/new/aboutjordan/ph3.shtml. (11589)

22. For this and a host of other quotes from Arab spokespersons on the Syrian identity of local Arabs, see: www.yahoodi.com/peace/palestinians.html. (11921)

23. See Jim Gerrish, *The Lie of the Land or How to Steal a Heritage*, Church & Israel Forum, at: www.churchisraelforum.com/the_lie_of_the_land.htm. (11570)

24. See: Article 25 in the "Mandate for Palestine."

25. See: The Charter of the United Nations at: http://middleeastfacts.org/content/UN-documents/ UN_Charter_One_Document.htm. (11032)

26. See Eugene V. Rostow, *The Future of Palestine*, Institute for National Strategic Studies, November 1993. Professor Rostow was Sterling Professor of Law and Public Affairs Emeritus at Yale University and served as the Dean of Yale Law School (1955-66); Distinguished Research Professor of Law and Diplomacy, National Defense University; Adjunct Fellow, American Enterprise Institute. In 1967, as U.S. Under-Secretary of State for Political Affairs, he became a key draftee of UN Resolution 242. See also his article: *Are Israel's Settlements Legal? The New Republic*, October 21, 1991.
27. See: Judge, Sir Elihu Lauterpacht, *Jerusalem and the Holy Places* (London: The Anglo-Israel Association, 1968).
28. *Ibid.*
29. Report of the High Commissioner on the Administration of Palestine 1920-1925, Jerusalem, April 22, 1925, p. 24-25.
30. Palestine Royal Commission Report, July 1937, Chapter II, p. 31.
31. Palestine Royal Commission Report, July 1937, Chapter II, p. 24.
32. Palestine Royal Commission Report, July 1937, Chapter II, p. 31.
33. ICJ - International status of South West Africa. Advisory Opinion of July 11, 1950. See at: www.mefacts.com/cached.asp?x_id=10954. (10954)
34. Legal consequences for states of the continued presence of South Africa in Namibia (South West Africa) notwithstanding Security Council Resolution 276 (1970). International Court of Justice, Advisory Opinion of June 21, 1971 (paras. 42-86) states: "The last resolution of the League Assembly and Article 80, paragraph 1, of the United Nations Charter maintained the obligations of mandatories. The International Court of Justice has consistently recognized that the Mandate survived the demise of the League."
35. Advisory Opinion of July 9, 2004, paragraph 49. See: www.mefacts.com/cache/html/icj/10908.htm. (10908)
36. Eugene V. Rostow, *The Future of Palestine*. Adapted from the paper delivered at the American Leadership Conference on Israel and the Middle East on October 10, 1993 in Arlington, Virginia.
37. *Ibid.*
38. United Nations 1922 Census. See: www.unu.edu/unupress/unupbooks/80859e/80859E05.htm. (11373)
39. Palestine Royal Report, July 1937, Chapter II, p. 28, paragraph 29.
40. See Paragraph 70 in the ICJ Advisory Opinion, July 9, 2004.
41. A Class "A" mandate assigned to Britain was Iraq, and assigned to France were Syria and Lebanon. Examples of other types of mandates were the Class "B" mandate assigned to Belgium administering Ruanda-Urundi, and the Class "C" mandate assigned to South Africa administering South West Africa.
42. Palestine Royal Report, July 1937, Chapter II, p. 38.
43. *Ibid.* p. 39.
44. *Ibid.* p. 40.
45. See Appendix C: Article 22 of the Covenant of the League of Nations.
46. Palestine Royal Report, July 1937, Chapter II, p. 38.
47. The Peace Treaty of Sèvres, August 10, 1920. www.mefacts.com/cache/html/mandate/11460.htm. (11460)
48. See the full text of the "Mandate" in Appendix A.
49. Palestine Royal Report, July 1937, Chapter II, p. 20.